I0817136

Pinto Horses

by Grace Hansen

Abdo Kids Jumbo is an Imprint of Abdo Kids
abdobooks.com

abdobooks.com

Published by Abdo Kids, a division of ABDO, P.O. Box 398166, Minneapolis, Minnesota 55439.

Abdo Kids Jumbo™ is a trademark and logo of Abdo Kids.

Printed in the United States of America, North Mankato, Minnesota.

052019

092019

Photo Credits: Alamy, AP Images, Depositphotos Enterprise, iStock, Shutterstock

Production Contributors: Teddy Borth, Jennie Forsberg, Grace Hansen
Design Contributors: Dorothy Toth, Pakou Moua

Library of Congress Control Number: 2018963346

Publisher's Cataloging-in-Publication Data

Names: Hansen, Grace, author.

Title: Pinto horses / by Grace Hansen.

Description: Minneapolis, Minnesota : Abdo Kids, 2020 | Series: Horses set 2 | Includes online resources and index.

Identifiers: ISBN 9781532185670 (lib. bdg.) | ISBN 9781532186653 (ebook) | ISBN 9781532187148 (Read-to-me ebook)

Subjects: LCSH: Pinto horse--Juvenile literature. | Calico horse--Juvenile literature. | Horses--Juvenile literature.

Classification: DDC 636.13--dc23

Table of Contents

Pinto Horses

Pinto horses are easy to spot. That's because they have large spots!

Pinto is not a breed of horse. It is a coat **pattern**. Pintos can be any kind of horse.

Pinto horses have pink skin. Their eyes are often light blue in color.

Markings

Pintos can have all white or multicolored **hooves**.

Pinto horses have coats with large patches of white. They have two main **patterns**.

Overero pintos have white coloring that spreads up from the belly. This is mixed with a darker color.

Tobiano pintos have white that spreads down from the back. This **pattern** is smoother and more regular than overo.

Pinto Breeds

Pintos can be **draft horses**. Gypsy horses are great for pulling carts.

Tennessee walking horses can have pinto coloring. They are great for saddle riding.

More Facts

- The pinto was often used as a war horse. Its coloring was thought to be helpful because it acted like a natural **camouflage**.

- Pintos that are **stock horses** are most often Quarter horses.

- The Pinto Horse Association of America formed in 1956. More than 100,000 pinto horses are **registered** with the group.

Glossary

camouflage – way of hiding something by coloring so that it looks like its surroundings.

draft horse – a large horse used for pulling heavy loads, especially a cart or plow.

hoof – the hard, tough covering on the feet of certain mammals such as horses.

pattern – an arrangement of shapes and colors.

registered – to be on an official list or record.

stock horse – a horse that is trained to herd livestock.

Index